The Box

I Talk You Talk Press

Copyright © 2019 I Talk You Talk Press

ISBN: 978-4-909733-27-6

www.italkyoutalk.com

info@italkyoutalk.com

All rights reserved. No part of this publication may be resold, reproduced, stored in retrieval system, copied in any form or by any means, electronic, mechanical, photocopying, recording or otherwise transmitted without the prior written permission from the publisher. You must not circulate this publication in any format, online or otherwise.

This is a work of fiction. Names, characters, businesses, organizations, products, places, events and incidents are either the products of the author's imagination or are used in a fictitious manner. We have no affiliation with any existing companies mentioned in this story. Any resemblance to actual persons, living or dead, existing stories or actual events is purely coincidental.

Although the author and publisher have made every effort to ensure that the contents of this book were correct at press time, the author and publisher do not assume and hereby disclaim any liability to any party for any loss, damage, or disruption caused by errors or omissions, whether such errors or omissions result from negligence, accident, or any other cause.

For more information, see the Copyright Notice on our website.

Image copyright: © pauchi #102923601 Adobe Stock Standard license

CONTENTS

1. Alice — 1
2. Darryl — 3
3. Lisa — 5
4. The box — 7
5. Old history — 10
6. The next morning — 12
7. Gabby — 15
8. The paintings — 18
9. A day out — 20
10. The gallery — 23
11. Clothes — 25
12. Gerry Wallace — 28
13. Shopping — 31

14. Ralph	34
15. An apology	37
16. An unexpected present	40
17. Elizabeth	42
18. Ralph's story	46
19. Waiting	49
20. A plan for the meeting	52
21. Gerry's story	55
22. Shocked	58
23. Four months later	61
Thank You	62
About the Author	63

1. ALICE

Lisa sat next to the bed in the quiet room. The room was painted white. The windows were open, and the white curtains moved in the breeze. The birds were singing. The sun was starting to warm the garden. Soon the heat of the sun would create fragrance from the spring flowers.

But Lisa was focussed on the woman in the bed. It was her mother, Alice. For more than three weeks, Lisa had come every day to sit with her mother. Her mother was dying. Most evenings, Lisa went home and her mother's sister, Lisa's aunt, Yvonne, came to sit with the dying woman.

But, around midnight, a nurse had called Lisa at home.

"I think you should come soon," she said. "Your mother will die tomorrow. We cannot help her anymore."

Lisa went to the hospital and sat with her mother. The day before, her mother was able to talk, but now it was close to the end. Her mother could not talk. Lisa held her mother's hand.

Her mother's eyes opened. She was staring at Lisa.

No, thought Lisa. *She is not looking at me. She is looking at something else.*

Lisa followed her mother's eyes. Her mother was looking at a box.

That old box! What is it doing here in the hospital? Who brought it here?

Lisa remembered the box very well. It was made from wood. It had carvings of elephants on it. Lisa thought it was from India. Lisa's mother put sewing things in it. Needles, thread, scissors…. But why was it here? Why was it in the hospital room of a dying woman?

Lisa's mother could not talk, but her eyes could speak.

What does she want? Lisa asked herself. *Something in the box?*

Lisa walked to the box and brought it back to the bed.

"This box. Is it important?" she asked her mother.

Her mother's eyes said 'yes'.

"Do you want me to take the box?"

Again, her mother's eyes said 'yes'.

"OK. I will take the box."

Lisa held her mother's hand.

Her mother seemed to have new strength. She held Lisa's hand tightly. She spoke. She said one word, "Sorry."

Then, her hand relaxed.

Lisa rang the bell next to bed.

The nurse came in.

"I think she's gone," said Lisa. She stood up and walked to the window.

The nurse went to the bed and checked.

"Yes, I'm sorry," said the nurse. "Alice has died. Can I call someone for you?"

"Yes," said Lisa. "I will call my aunt, but could you please call my husband? Will you ask him to come and get me? I want to go home."

"OK," said the nurse. "I'll leave you with your mother now. I'll come and get you when your husband arrives."

"Just one thing," said Lisa. "When did that box come here? It has always been in my mother's bedroom. I didn't bring it here."

"Your aunt brought it here last night. She said your mother had asked for it. Your aunt went to your mother's apartment and brought it here. I don't know why."

"Thank you," said Lisa. "I'll take it away with me."

She went back to the hospital bed and sat staring at her mother until it was time to go.

2. DARRYL

It was the day after the funeral. Lisa was sitting at the kitchen table. She was reading sympathy cards and messages. The carved wooden box sat on the table. Lisa had taken out the threads, scissors and needles, and put them in a drawer.

My mother had this box as long as I can remember. I will keep all these lovely cards and messages in it.

She could hear her husband Darryl moving around upstairs. There was a lot of banging and thumping.

I wonder what he is doing? She smiled. *He is such a good husband. He helped me with everything for the funeral. He was always there when it was difficult.*

She heard Darryl walking down the stairs. He came into the kitchen.

"Look at this lovely card," she said. "It's from the Watkins. They used to live next door to my mother, but they live in Australia now, and couldn't come to the funeral."

"I have to talk to you," said Darryl. Lisa looked at him. He was wearing his jacket.

"Are you going out?"

"No. I'm leaving. I've packed most of my clothes. I will come back and take other things from the house later, but I'm leaving today."

Lisa didn't understand. "Leaving? Where are you going?"

Darryl was still standing by the door. "I have fallen in love with another woman. I am going to live with her. I want a divorce. Then I will marry her."

"What? What do you mean? When did you meet her?"

"I met her a few months ago."

"And you didn't tell me?" Lisa was shouting.

"Well. I didn't think it would last. She is much younger than me. I couldn't believe such a beautiful young woman would want to stay with me. Her name is Kathy. Would you like to see a photograph?" Darryl put his hand into his pocket.

"Are you crazy? Do you want me to tell you how beautiful she is and how lucky you are?"

Darryl went red. "No. I guess not. That was a stupid idea. But I have to explain. We realised about a month ago that we were in love. I wanted to tell you then. I wanted to leave you then. But your mother was dying. I thought it would be too difficult for you. So we waited."

"And you don't think this is a difficult time now?"

"Well, we don't want to wait any longer. You see, we have amazing news. Kathy is pregnant. We're going to have a baby."

Lisa felt a pain like a knife in her heart. She had always wanted children, but they had not been lucky. Now she was over forty, and it was too late.

Darryl was still talking. "I talked to a lawyer. You will need your own lawyer. I will give you a little money for a while, but then you will need a job. This house must be sold as soon as possible. Kathy and I want to buy a house and have everything ready for when our baby comes. I'm going now. Kathy is waiting for me."

He walked out of the kitchen.

Lisa couldn't speak. She heard him open the front door, and watched through the window as he carried two big bags to the car.

She wanted to run out and scream, "Come back! Come back!" But she couldn't move.

3. LISA

For the next few weeks, Lisa felt like a sleepwalker. Aunt Yvonne helped her a lot. She was over 70, but she was still a successful businesswoman with a popular fashion boutique in the city. She found Lisa a good lawyer. She organized everything, and told Lisa what to do. Lisa agreed with everything. She had no energy to argue with Aunt Yvonne, or anyone else.

She spent most of her time sitting in the kitchen. A friend of Kathy's wanted to buy the house, so it happened very quickly. Lisa realised that Darryl had been planning everything for weeks. Darryl came to the house often. He always sent a text to say when he would come. Lisa always went out when he was coming to the house. She didn't want to see him, or talk to him. She sat in coffee shops and tried not to think about anything.

Darryl would text to say he was leaving, and then Lisa would walk, or take a bus back to the house. She didn't trust herself to drive.

I am like a crazy person. I am half asleep all the time. I might have an accident and kill someone.

Every time she went back to the house, more things would be gone – furniture, books, a television. The house felt strange and empty.

Finally, it was moving day. Aunt Yvonne had found an apartment for Lisa in a new building near the centre of the city. The moving company came and took the furniture.

When Lisa left the house, she was carrying the wooden box. Her world had fallen apart, and this box seemed to be the only link with a happier past.

4. THE BOX

Aunt Yvonne was waiting at Lisa's new apartment. She had got the moving company to arrange all the furniture. She had unpacked most of the kitchen stuff, and filled the bookcase. There was a bottle of champagne and glasses on the table.

"Now sit down, Lisa," she said. "We are going to drink to your future. Your new life."

Lisa put the box on the table and sat down. She looked around the new apartment. It had an open-plan kitchen/living/dining area and one bedroom. The few pieces of furniture from her old house looked strange. She had the table she was sitting at, a small sofa, and a coffee table. Aunt Yvonne had done a wonderful job, but to Lisa, everything looked wrong. Tears ran down her face.

"I don't want a new life! I want my old life back!"

Aunt Yvonne was shocked. "Lisa! You don't want that rat Darryl back!"

"Yes I do. I was happy. Now everything has gone wrong!"

Aunt Yvonne sat down at the table. "No. You thought you were happy. Maybe you were for a while, but Darryl wasn't happy, was he?"

"Yes he was! I did everything for him. I didn't go out with friends. I didn't get a job! I was always waiting for him. I was a good wife! I was! Why did it go wrong?"

"Maybe he didn't want a good wife," said Aunt Yvonne. "You must move on. What are you going to do? Get a job?"

"I will have to find a job. I have half of the money from the house, and Darryl is going to give me a little money for about six weeks. But if I don't have a job in six weeks, I will have to use the money from selling the house. It won't last long. I still have to pay the lawyer and the moving company. Can I come and work in your shop?"

Aunt Yvonne opened the champagne and poured some into the two glasses. She handed one to Lisa.

"No" she said. "Your clothes and hair are all wrong. My boutique is very fashionable. You have the wrong image."

Lisa drank the champagne in her glass without thinking.

Aunt Yvonne poured some more from the bottle.

"I could get a make-over," said Lisa.

Her aunt stared at her. "Yes, you could. It would be a very good idea. I will help you. But you still can't work for me."

Lisa was angry. This was good. For weeks she had not felt angry, just sad. "Why not?" she asked.

"You're too quiet. You're depressed. Who would buy expensive clothes from you? I need smiles and energy and personality. Not someone who looks half asleep and cries all the time. Now you must make a plan. What job would you like to do? Would you like to work in a library?"

Lisa cried and cried. "I don't know!"

Oh dear, thought Yvonne. *We must talk about something else.*

"I see you have Alice's box," she said. "You know she asked me to collect it and take it to the hospital. I don't know why. Did she tell you why she wanted it?"

"No," said Lisa. "It was in her room the day she died, but she wasn't speaking by then. Oh, that's not true. She said one word, 'Sorry'. It seemed to have something to do with box."

"I remember when Alice got that box," said Yvonne. "Do you remember the secret drawer?"

"No. I never knew there was a secret drawer."

"Alice showed it to me. Maybe I can remember how it works. Give me the box."

Lisa handed the box to Yvonne.

She put it on the table in front of her. "Now, let me think."

It took Yvonne a long time, but finally she worked it out. There was a click, and a shallow drawer slid out from the bottom of the box. Inside was an envelope. The paper of the envelope was yellow and stained. As Yvonne lifted it out, the paper cracked, and small pieces fell on the table.

Yvonne handed the envelope to Lisa and poured herself some more wine.

"Maybe Alice wanted you to find this."

5. OLD HISTORY

Lisa's hands were shaking. She tried to open the envelope, but the paper was so old that the envelope broke and the contents fell out.

There was only an old photograph and a small brass ring.

Lisa picked up the photograph and stared at it. It showed a young man and woman. They were dressed in jeans and shirts. The woman had very long hair. Her face was alive with joy. The man had a long hair too, and a beard.

"Is that my mother?" Yvonne walked around the table and looked over Lisa's shoulder. "Yes. That's Alice. She looks like she is about twenty years old."

"But who is the man in the photograph?" asked Lisa. "It's not my father."

"No. I think that's Gerry. Yes. I'm sure that's Gerry."

"Who was he?"

Yvonne frowned. "It was all a long time ago, and your mother was younger than me. I think I was living in Auckland with my first husband at the time. Anyway, he was Alice's boyfriend at university. Maybe she only went to university for two years, and then she quit. Well, Gerry and Alice were into drugs, peace and spiritual ideas. They went to India. Our parents, your grandparents, were so angry, but they went. After about a year, Alice came back to New Zealand. She came with your father. She was pregnant and they got married very quickly. You were born about six months later."

Yvonne looked at the photograph again. "She was really beautiful, wasn't she? Alice got the looks and I got the style."

Lisa was puzzled. "I guess so. But why did my mother want me to have this photograph? And what is important about this ring?"

"I don't know," said Yvonne. "It's late. You're tired. I'm tired. I have to go to work tomorrow." She stood up. "I'm going home. Enjoy your new apartment. I've made the bed for you. I didn't have time to unpack all the boxes, so that will be a job for you tomorrow.

"I've put food in the refrigerator. There's milk, fruit and margarine. I bought a quiche from the bakery too. Make sure you eat before you go to bed. I put some bread and other things in the pantry. Come and have coffee with me tomorrow. No, not tomorrow. I will be busy. The next day."

Yvonne kissed her niece on the cheek, and went out the door.

Lisa poured herself some more champagne from the bottle.

I'll finish the bottle and then I'll go to bed. Maybe if I'm drunk, I will sleep.

6. THE NEXT MORNING

It was almost 10:30 when Lisa woke the next morning. She had fallen asleep on top of the bed. She was still wearing her clothes from the day before. She felt terrible. She went to the kitchen and drank a glass of water. The coffeemaker was on the kitchen counter. She found coffee in the pantry and started the coffeemaker. Then she went to the bathroom. Yvonne had somehow found enough time to unpack Lisa's bathroom box.

She is amazing, thought Lisa. *But then there wasn't very much.*

She looked at her beauty products. Soap, shampoo, conditioner, face cream and body cream from the supermarket, and toothpaste.

What am I doing thinking about my beauty products? I need a shower. Now!

Lisa pulled off her clothes and got under the shower. She washed her hair, and stayed under the water until it went cold.

Oh no! This apartment is expensive, and I can only have a twenty-minute shower!

Lisa wrapped a towel around her body and went back to the bedroom. It took her 10 minutes to find underwear, jeans and a T-shirt in the boxes of clothes.

With a towel wrapped around her wet hair, Lisa dressed. The smell of coffee was wonderful. She found a coffee mug in one of the kitchen cupboards, and took her coffee to the table. Lisa drank her coffee. She went back to the kitchen and poured herself another mug. She made some toast and took her breakfast back to the table.

The room was very bright and warm. The furniture didn't look so bad today.

The Box

If I get some flowers and hang some pictures, maybe it will look better, thought Lisa. *But not today. Why did I drink all that champagne last night? And why didn't I eat something? I am not surprised I feel so ill this morning.*

The torn envelope, photograph and ring were still on the table. Lisa picked up the envelope.

I can throw this away. But why did my mother keep these things? I don't understand. I think she was trying to tell me something. 'Sorry'. What was she sorry for? Was she saying sorry to me, or did she want me to tell someone else she was sorry?

There was nothing written on the outside of the envelope, but Lisa realised there was still something inside.

She pulled out a piece of paper. It was a story from a newspaper. It was about a special programme for city kids. Children who were not doing well at school and causing trouble, were sent to a camp in Northland. They learned new skills, and experienced farm life and outdoor life for a month during the summer holidays. The reporter had written that the programme was very successful. The children became more confident, and when they went back to school, their teachers said they studied better, and caused less trouble in the classroom.

The programme was run by a man called Gerry Wallace. There was a picture of him. Lisa picked up the photograph from the box and put it next to the photograph in the newspaper story. The man in the newspaper had short hair and no beard, but Lisa thought it might be the same person.

She put everything back into the box.

Too much mystery for a woman with a hangover, she thought. *I have to start my new life. So today I'll unpack my clothes, and the other boxes Aunt Yvonne didn't open.*

Lisa worked hard for the rest of the day. She unpacked her clothes and put them away.

She had a few paintings she had bought before she was married. They had been stored in the garage because Darryl didn't like them. She put them under her bed.

I'll hang them up when I am feeling more creative, she thought.

She unpacked the other boxes of pots and pans, and more books. She found a box full of photograph albums.

My life with Darryl. Our wedding photographs!

She closed the box, and pushed it into the back of a cupboard.

It was late when she finally finished. She collapsed all the cardboard boxes and tied them with some string.

I'm too tired to do any more.

Lisa ate the quiche from the refrigerator, drank a glass of water, and went to bed.

7. GABBY

Lisa woke early. For the first time in months, she felt good. She made coffee, and sat at the table planning her day.

Coffee with Aunt Yvonne. Then I'll go to the hardware store and buy some picture hooks. I'll need a hammer too. Darryl took all the tools. I need to go grocery shopping too.

Her mobile phone beeped. It was a text message from Aunt Yvonne.

--- Sorry can't make it for coffee today. Will call later. ---

Lisa was disappointed. It would have been nice to see her aunt.

I haven't thanked her for all her help and hard work. And I'd like to ask her more about Gerry. Maybe she remembers his family name. I'd like to know if it is the same man who was in the newspaper story.

Lisa showered and dressed. She made breakfast and cleaned her apartment. It didn't take very long. Then she found the keys to the apartment and put them in her pocket. She took the bundle of cardboard boxes down to the recycling area in the basement of the apartment building. There was another woman there. She was emptying a bag filled with plastics into the plastics bin.

"Hi," said the woman. "Are you new? I haven't seen you before."

"Yes," said Lisa. "I moved into an apartment on the second floor two days ago."

The woman folded her bag and put it in the bin with the other plastics. She walked over to Lisa.

"I'm Gabby. I live on the top floor. I'm quite new too. We moved here from Auckland, six weeks ago."

"I'm Lisa."

Lisa put the bundle of cardboard into the paper-recycling bin. Gabby and Lisa climbed back up the stairs together.

"I'm a web-site designer so I work from home," said Gabby. "What do you do?"

"I don't have a job," said Lisa. "But I'm going to look for one."

Lisa stopped at her apartment door, and took her keys from her pocket.

"Would you like to come in for a coffee?" she asked Gabby.

"I'd love to!" answered Gabby.

Gabby sat at the table while Lisa made coffee. "Your apartment is a lot tidier than ours," she said. "My husband makes videos. He's in the Solomon Islands making a travel documentary. I'm always lazy when he's away. I haven't done any housework, so the apartment is a mess."

"I want to hang some pictures and make this room more interesting," said Lisa from the kitchen. "I think it looks boring and the furniture doesn't look right."

"I'll come and help you," said Gabby. "I like doing things like that, and it is more fun with two."

Lisa brought the coffee to the table. "I'm going to buy a hammer and some picture hooks today. So maybe tomorrow, if you have some free time?"

"Sure," said Gabby. She looked at the box on the table. "Nice box! Where did you get it?"

Lisa's eyes filled with tears. "It was my mother's. She died about a month ago."

Gabby reached out across the table and touched Lisa's hand. "I'm sorry. It must be a hard time for you. Were you living with your mother? Is that why you have moved here?"

Lisa was usually very shy, but Gabby was so friendly and nice. She told her about her mother, Darryl, Kathy and the baby.

"Oh, no!" said Gabby. "It is all too much for one person. I am sure you must feel lonely sometimes. I am always upstairs. You must come up any time you are feeling bad."

"Thank you," said Lisa. "But my Aunt Yvonne says I must get on with my life. You will not want me knocking on your door and disturbing you."

"Nonsense!" said Gabby. "I am living alone right now. I will enjoy having someone to talk to." She looked at her mobile phone. "But now I have to go. I have a deadline. So I must do some work. What time shall I come to help you hang pictures tomorrow?"

"About ten? Would that be good for you?"

"Sure. See you then. Give me your phone number. If I have to change the plan, I will text you."

They exchanged phone numbers and then Gabby left. Lisa took the coffee cups to the kitchen.

It's a long time since I had a friend, she thought. *Gabby is so nice. I hope we will be friends.*

Lisa ate lunch and went shopping. She bought food and flowers at the supermarket. She went to the hardware store and bought picture hooks and a hammer.

Aunt Yvonne called when Lisa was making a pasta sauce for dinner.

"I'm sorry I couldn't meet you today. I had an unexpected meeting."

"That's OK," said Lisa. "I know how busy you are."

"How are you?" asked Yvonne. "Are you OK?"

"Yes. I'm OK. I am feeling a little better. I went shopping. And I met one of my neighbours. She lives upstairs. We had coffee. She is coming tomorrow to help me hang some paintings on the walls."

"That's good." Yvonne was pleased. She was very worried about Lisa. "I'm going to Sydney tomorrow to buy clothes to sell in the boutique. I'll be back next week. I'll call you and text you from Sydney, but I'm pleased you have some plans."

"I'll be fine," said Lisa. "Don't worry about me. I hope you have a good trip."

8. THE PAINTINGS

The next morning, Lisa took the paintings from under her bed. She unwrapped them and put them on the floor in her living room.

When Gabby arrived, Lisa served coffee, but Gabby didn't sit down. She walked around the room looking at the paintings on the floor.

"I'm surprised," she said. "I didn't think you would have artwork like this."

Lisa laughed. "What kind of paintings did you think I would have?"

Gabby laughed too. "I don't know. Maybe very traditional ones? Pictures of lakes and mountains? Quite boring. I'm sorry, but I thought your pictures would be conservative, like your furniture. But these are amazing! You have very good taste."

"Well, my husband didn't think so," said Lisa. "I bought these before I was married. He hated them, so they stayed in the garage."

Gabby came to sit at the table and picked up her coffee. She stared at Lisa. "You look very conservative. Your hair. Your clothes. But maybe you aren't."

Lisa looked at Gabby. She was about the same age as Lisa. She was slim. Her hair was cut very short and it was dyed white. She was wearing flat shoes, leggings and a big shirt. She was wearing big bright wooden earrings and a matching necklace.

Lisa looked down at her clothes. Her brown pants and dark green T-shirt did not look good. Her black running shoes were like men's shoes.

Darryl never wanted me to wear bright fashionable clothes. He said I should dress to suit my age. He said that housewives should look like housewives. Well, I am not a wife anymore. Maybe I can change my look?

"My aunt said my clothes and hair are all wrong. I asked her if I could work in her shop but she said I have the wrong image."

Gabby was interested. "Your aunt has a shop?"

"Yes. A fashion boutique. It's called 'Yvonne's'."

"Oh, I know that one. It's very expensive. I don't shop there. It's too high class for me."

"My aunt said she would help me with a makeover."

"It's a good idea. It will cheer you up." Gabby put down her coffee cup. "Now, pictures! I have to finish a job today, so I have about two hours before I have to go back to work."

When Gabby left, Lisa sat and looked around the room. The bright abstract paintings on the walls made the room come alive. Lisa couldn't find her flower vases, so the irises she had bought from the supermarket were in a glass jar. The bright yellows and purples added another patch of colour. The room was brighter. Lisa felt happier.

This is my room, she thought. *I never thought about it, but Darryl always decided what furniture and decorations we would have. I always agreed with him. But now I can choose for myself. I wish there was enough wall space for the biggest painting. But never mind. I will put it back under the bed. And maybe six paintings in such a small room is enough.*

9. A DAY OUT

The next morning there was a text message from Gabby.

--- *Things to do today. But I'm free tomorrow if you are. I have a plan. We're going out. Come to my apartment at 8:00* ---

When Lisa rang the bell of Gabby's apartment the next morning, Gabby picked up her denim jacket and a bright red shoulder bag from a table just inside the door.

"Let's go! We'll take my car."

As they walked down to the car park, Lisa asked, "Are we going anywhere special?"

"Yes! We're going to have a day of luxury! We're going to the new beauty spa just out of town. Eight hours of massages, facials, manicures and pedicures!"

Lisa stopped on the stairs. "But Gabby! That will cost a lot of money! I don't have a job and I don't have much money!"

Gabby laughed. "Yes. It is a very expensive place. But I made their webpage for them. They were very pleased with the work I did. They gave me a voucher, for me and a friend. We don't have to pay anything!"

The new beauty spa was a wonderful place. The two women had a great day. The voucher included lunch. They sat at a small table on a terrace. They were wrapped up in towelling robes and were eating salads. The waitress brought them a small glass of white wine each.

Lisa looked out over the beautiful gardens to a small lake.

"Gabby! Thank you! I have never done anything like this before. It's magic. I loved the steam bath, the massage and the facial."

"Me too," said Gabby. "Then this afternoon we'll have manicures and pedicures, while they do our hair. I don't want to change my style so I will just ask for a hair treatment. What kind of hairstyle will you choose?"

"The same, I guess," said Lisa. "I don't have any ideas."

Gabby stared at Lisa. "Where do you usually go to have your hair cut?"

Lisa went red. "I always cut it myself."

"What! Are you crazy? No wonder it looks so ordinary! Oh. Sorry. That was rude. You have great hair, but it has no style. Tell the hairdresser you want something new."

"But I don't know what I want," said Lisa.

"OK. Tell the hairdresser you trust her. Ask her to pick a style that will suit you."

As they drove back into the city, Gabby was very quiet. Lisa wondered what was wrong. Then Gabby said, "Hmm. I've been thinking. Your new hairstyle is amazing! You look great. But your clothes are all wrong. It is rude to ask, but do you have any money?"

Lisa tried to explain. "My mother got sick about three years ago. She sold the house, and moved into a tiny apartment in a place that cares for old people. She wasn't so old, but she couldn't look after herself. It was very expensive. By the time she died, there was no money left.

"I will get half the money from the house Darryl and I lived in. It has been sold, but I don't have the money yet. Darryl is giving me a little money now, but that will stop in a few weeks. I have to pay the lawyer and the moving people. They are very kind. They will wait until I have the house money. Aunt Yvonne lent me the money to get into the apartment, but I have to pay her back.

"My husband didn't want me to work after we got married. So I don't have a job, and I don't have any experience. It might take me a long time to find a job, so I have to be very careful. "

"You could sell one of your paintings."

"Oh Gabby! They are not worth any money. I bought them from new artists. They were very cheap. I bought them because I liked them."

"Yes. But some of those artists might be famous now. Why don't you sell the biggest one? The one that was too big for the room?"

"I'll think about it."

They arrived back at their apartment building. Lisa hugged Gabby. "Thank you for a wonderful day!"

"I had a great time too," said Gabby. "I am going away tomorrow for three days. Think about selling the painting. We'll talk when I get back."

10. THE GALLERY

The next three days passed slowly for Lisa. She went for walks, read, and watched television. She sent cheerful answers to Aunt Yvonne's texts, but she missed Gabby.

Every time she looked in a mirror, she saw a stranger. She loved her new hairstyle. She looked like a different person.

A different person on the outside, she thought. *But I am still the same person on the inside.*

On the third day, she took the big painting out from under the bed.

Gabby will ask me if I am going to sell it. Maybe I should.

She wrapped it up carefully and carried it down to her car. Her car was very old.

I will have to buy another one. If I get some money for this painting, I should save it. I shouldn't spend money on clothes.

Lisa drove to an art gallery in the city. She carried the painting inside and explained to the woman at reception that she wanted to sell it.

"I don't know if it is worth anything," she said. "Maybe no one will want to buy it."

The woman called to a young man in the room behind her.

"Please take this painting into the meeting room." She smiled at Lisa. "I'll call Ralph Watt to come and look at it. He is the owner of this gallery."

The young man carried the painting into a room with a large table. He unwrapped the painting and put it on a stand in the corner of the room. He said, "Ralph will be here soon. Please wait."

Very soon, a man came into the room. He was about Lisa's age. He was tall and thin. He was wearing jeans and a checked shirt. Lisa was surprised.

I thought the owner of an art gallery would wear smart clothes, she thought.

He saw the painting and walked over to it. He looked at it for a long time. Then he turned to Lisa and said, "Is this yours? Where did you get it?"

"I bought it from the artist about twenty-five years ago."

"Really! And now you want to sell it! Why?" asked Ralph.

"I have moved into a small apartment. There is no room for it."

"I see. Well, I can sell it very easily. Or you could send it to an auction of New Zealand art. I can help you do that."

"Oh, but I need money now. I can't wait very long."

"I can put it in the gallery for you. But to be truthful, I would like to buy it for myself. Did you know the artist is dead now?"

"No, I didn't."

"Yes. He died last year. This is a very special and important painting. I will pay you fifteen thousand dollars for it. But if you send it to an auction, many people will want to buy it. You might get a lot more money."

Lisa was very surprised. "Fifteen thousand dollars? But I only paid a hundred and fifty dollars! I bought it because I liked it."

Ralph Watt laughed. "Then you were very lucky, or you have a talent for choosing good art. Are you sure you want to sell it?"

Lisa sat down on one of the chairs next to the meeting table. "Yes! I want to sell it. I want to sell it to you."

Lisa drove back to her apartment without the painting. She had waited while Ralph transferred $15,000 into her bank account. She still couldn't believe it.

I can buy a good second-hand car and still have money to buy some clothes! I can't wait to tell Gabby!

11. CLOTHES

Lisa got a text from Gabby the next day.

--- *I'm back. Coffee?* ---

Lisa was very pleased to see her friend. They drank coffee while Gabby told Lisa about her trip. Then she said, "Do you have something to tell me? What is it?"

Lisa laughed. "Yes, you're right!" She told Gabby about the painting and the money. "So I can save most of the money to buy another car, and I can buy myself something new. Maybe I can go to Yvonne's, and buy a new outfit."

"No! No!" said Gabby. "Don't go there! I know it is your aunt's shop, but it is too expensive. You need a whole new set of clothes. You could spend all the money from the painting at your aunt's shop, and still not have enough clothes! I will take you shopping. We need to make a plan! We will need a whole day, so maybe tomorrow or the day after."

She jumped up from the table. "Let's go and look at your clothes now. I am sure you should give most of them to a charity for old ladies!"

Lisa got very tired and depressed, because Gabby looked at all her clothes saying, "No. No. No!"

Gabby was excited, but Lisa needed a rest.

"Can you stay for lunch?" she asked. "I'll make an omelette."

"Yes please! I haven't been to the supermarket since I got back."

Lisa went to the kitchen and made lunch. Gabby came out of Lisa's bedroom and said, "I found two sweaters and a jacket you can keep, but…."

"Calm down and eat!" laughed Lisa. "Can you set the table?"

Gabby started to set the table. The wooden box was still on the table. "Where shall I put this?" she asked.

"I don't know," said Lisa. "I haven't found a good place for it yet."

Lisa didn't feel like talking about how bad her clothes were, or how many new things she should buy. While they ate their omelettes and salad, she told Gabby about the box and its secret drawer.

Gabby was very interested. After lunch, Lisa took the ring, the photograph and the newspaper article out of the box and showed them to Gabby.

"Is this your mother?" she asked. She pointed to the woman in the photograph.

"Yes," said Lisa.

"You look a lot like her," said Gabby.

"Oh, no! Aunt Yvonne said she was beautiful. And she was. Until she got sick, she was a very beautiful woman."

Oh, Lisa, thought Gabby. *You are beautiful. If you had more confidence and better clothes, everyone would look at you. What happened to you?*

"Have you googled this guy, Gerry Wallace?" she asked Lisa.

"No. I don't have a computer."

"Why didn't you go to an Internet café?"

"I guess I just didn't think of it."

"Can you use a computer?"

"Oh, yes. Of course I can. There was a computer in our house. But Darryl said he needed it. So he and Kathy have it."

Gabby jumped up from the table. "I'll be back soon."

She ran up the stairs to her apartment.

That Darryl is so selfish. Why did Lisa let him take everything from the house? It's a good thing he didn't know how valuable that painting was. He would have taken that too!

Gabby soon returned to Lisa's apartment. She was carrying a small laptop computer. She put it on the table and switched it on. "The whole building has WIFI, so that's good. Where's that newspaper article? Can I have some coffee?"

Lisa put the newspaper article next to the computer, and went to make coffee.

She came back with two cups of coffee and watched Gabby

The Box

search the Internet.

Finally, Gabby sat back and took her coffee.

"Well, the newspaper story is about this programme for children with problems. The story was in the newspapers about thirty years ago. The programme finished about five years later.

"I looked for someone called Gerry Wallace. There are many people with that name. But the search is easier if we know he is a New Zealander. Do you think he is?"

"Maybe," said Lisa. "He met my mother at university here, so I guess so."

"Why don't you tidy up your bedroom? I left all your 'old-lady' clothes on the bed and on the floor. It will take me a while to do some more searching."

"But don't you have to work? Don't you have jobs for clients?"

"Yes, I do, but I will work later this afternoon and tonight. This is more interesting and important."

Lisa went out of the room.

I am so lucky to have a friend like Gabby, she thought. *But she is so energetic. Sometimes she does everything too quickly for me.*

She sighed and went to get some garbage bags.

I guess Gabby is right. My clothes are awful. I will take them to a charity shop.

12. GERRY WALLACE

About an hour later, Gabby came into Lisa's bedroom.

"I've done as much as I can today. I must go upstairs and do some work. But come and see what I found."

Lisa sat next to Gabby in front of the computer screen.

"I guessed that the Gerry Wallace we are looking for is aged between sixty and seventy. That made it much easier. There are only two that I can find. And here are their pictures," said Gabby.

Lisa stared at the pictures on the computer screen. One was a formal picture included in a profile of a Gerald Wallace's business interests. The other photograph was of a group of six people. The names of the people were under the photograph.

"That's the man in the photograph in the newspaper story," she said and pointed to a man in the group photograph. "But, I don't know if it's the same man who is in the photograph with my mother."

"I think it must be," said Gabby. "I have to go now. See what you can find out about him."

Gabby stood up and walked towards the door.

"But your computer," said Lisa. "You need your computer."

"I bought that one for my mother. She didn't like it. She said the screen was too small. You can use it for a while. I left you a note about how to connect to the WIFI in this building."

Lisa sat down and looked at the photograph. It had been taken at some kind of party. The people in the group were wearing casual clothes. They had glasses in their hands. They were all smiling at the

The Box

camera. Gabby had found it on a Facebook page. The comment next to the photograph said --- *Reunion party, summer 2017. First time we've all been together since 1992* ---

The page belonged to a woman called Elizabeth Benson. Lisa looked at Elizabeth's profile. She was 65. She lived in Raumati. Lisa knew Raumati well. It was a small coastal town about an hour's drive away from the city. Elizabeth was married. That was all Lisa could find out.

Why am I doing this? It's crazy. I am looking for a man in a photograph with my mother. The photograph is more than forty years old. It's a stupid thing to do.

But Lisa knew that her mother had wanted to tell her something, or show her something before she died. The photograph, the newspaper story, and the ring were the only clues. *I have to keep looking.*

Lisa looked up the online telephone directory for Raumati. She could not find anyone called Benson on the list. She went back and looked at the photograph again. She read the names of the people.

I don't believe it. One of them is Ralph Watt! The man I sold the picture to! I can call the auction house tomorrow and talk to him. Maybe he can tell me something. But I should be looking for a job.

Lisa searched for jobs on the Internet. It was very depressing. She found cafés that were looking for people to make coffee, waitresses and kitchen helpers, but they all wanted people with experience. She found advertisements for salespeople, but they wanted people with experience. Office positions needed experience and skills such as working with spreadsheets. It seemed the only options were housecleaning, or working in a gas station. Somehow, Lisa didn't want to get a job cleaning other people's houses. She had been a stay-at-home housewife all her married life. She wanted to do something different. Working in a gas station might be fun, but then Lisa thought she was too old to get that kind of job.

She sighed. *I will have to take a course and learn some skills. But then I might spend a lot of money on the course, and still not be able to find a job.*

Lisa's phone beeped. It was a text from Gabby.

--- *Can you be ready at 9:00am tomorrow? We're going shopping.* ---

Lisa wasn't pleased.

I want to call Ralph Watt. I don't want to spend a lot of money. Gabby doesn't understand how worried I am. I have to get a job, but I can't find one. She stopped and thought about it. *Gabby is so nice. She is a lot of fun. I*

am lucky to have her as a friend, and she only wants to help.
She sent a reply. --- *I'll be ready at 9:00.* ---

13. SHOPPING

Lisa lay on her sofa. It was 6:00pm and she was very tired. Gabby had taken her to discount stores, family clothes marts, second-hand shops and charity shops.

The floor was covered in shopping bags. Gabby had helped her carry everything in from the car, and then had disappeared.

"I have a Skype date with my husband," she said.

Lisa had bought four pairs of pants, a skirt, three dresses, a lot of T-shirts, a cardigan, a jacket, sandals, sneakers and shoes. It was amazing, but thanks to Gabby's clever shopping, it had all cost less than $500!

Gabby wouldn't let her buy anything in brown.

"You need bright colours. Not mud colours," she had said.

So all the clothes were in pinks, blues and turquoise. Gabby had found cheap, chunky earrings and necklaces, a crazy sunhat, a scarf and a swimsuit.

Lisa got off the sofa and made herself a cheese sandwich. She drank a coffee, and then carried the bags into her bedroom. She put the clothes out on the bed and smiled.

Gabby is so clever. When I tried these clothes on in the shops, I looked like a different person. I felt like a different person. Maybe my new life is really beginning. Tomorrow I'll wear one of these outfits. I'll call Ralph Watt and I'll call Aunt Yvonne. She should be back by tomorrow.

Then Lisa thought, *I can't wait. I'll change my clothes now.*

She put on her new jeans. They were very different from her old ones. "You must buy clothes that fit you!" Gabby had been very tough. Lisa chose a bright T-shirt and found a necklace of wooden beads and the earrings that matched them. She put on white sneakers, brushed her hair and looked in the mirror. *Yes! It's a new me!*

She heard the doorbell ring. *That will be Gabby. She'll be pleased I am already wearing my new clothes.*

Lisa hurried to the door. It was her aunt. Yvonne walked into the apartment.

"I can't stay long. I came here from the airport. I was worried about you. I've brought you a present. I know you like those boring browns and greens but …." Yvonne stopped talking.

She stared at Lisa. "What have you done to yourself? I've been away for ten days and you look like a different person!"

Lisa laughed. She kissed her aunt. "Do you have time for a cup of coffee or a glass of wine? I'll tell you about it."

Yvonne sat down. "Wine, please. I need it. You have given me quite a shock!"

Lisa brought wine, cheese and crackers to the table.

She told Yvonne the story. She explained about the visit to the beauty spa and the new hairstyle. She told her about selling the picture. Yvonne looked around the room.

"Well, your living space looks a lot better now. Those pictures make a big difference. And you bought all of them yourself? You are good at choosing art."

"So, I had a new hairstyle, but Gabby said my clothes were awful. We went shopping today for a new set of clothes…." Lisa stopped. She went red. "We didn't go to your shop, I'm sorry."

"Of course not. Everything is very expensive there. A new set of clothes? So you bought more?"

"Oh, yes. I bought a lot."

"Show me," said Yvonne.

Lisa took Yvonne into the bedroom.

Yvonne looked at all the clothes. She arranged them on the bed as different outfits. She looked pleased. "You and your friend did very well," she said.

"It wasn't me," answered Lisa. "All I did was try on a lot of different things and pay for them."

"And how much did you spend?"

"About five hundred dollars."

"Well, your friend has a real talent. I wonder if she would work for me?"

"No," laughed Lisa. "She is a web designer. She's not looking for a job."

"That's a pity. But never mind. Now, can you make me a coffee? I'll have a coffee with you, and then I must go home."

Yvonne sat at the table and watched Lisa while she made coffee.

I remember when she was young. She was a very pretty child. Then I didn't see her for years. By the time I came back here, she was married. She lost her energy. But now she's a different person. She has more energy. More personality. And she looks very attractive. Alice was beautiful. Lisa looks like her now. Yvonne's eyes filled with tears. *I miss you, Alice. I promise you, I will help Lisa. She has been unhappy for too long. Maybe I can help her be happy in life.*

When Lisa bought the coffee to the table, Yvonne said. "I bought you these in Sydney. I thought you mightn't like them, but I wanted you to have something pretty."

She handed a bag from an expensive store to Lisa. Inside were a gold and white shoulder bag and a silk scarf. The scarf was patterned with blue and white butterflies.

Lisa was delighted. "Oh, Aunt Yvonne, they're perfect." She jumped up and kissed her.

"Your friend has helped you buy a new set of clothes," said Yvonne. "Most things you have are very cheap, but if you add good accessories, no one will notice."

Yvonne drank her coffee and stood up. "I'm going now. Call me in a few days."

After Yvonne left, Lisa put her new clothes away, washed the dishes and got ready for bed.

Just before she went to sleep, Lisa thought, *I haven't thought about Darryl for two days. Aunt Yvonne liked my new look! And I forgot to tell her about the search for Gerry Wallace. Never mind. I can tell her another time.*

Lisa fell asleep with a smile on her face.

14. RALPH

The next morning, Lisa showered, and dressed in another new outfit. As she was cleaning her teeth after breakfast, she thought, *I must buy some skincare products and some makeup.*

She looked at the receipt from the art gallery. She called the number and asked to speak to Ralph Watt.

"He's not here," said the receptionist. "I will ask him to call you."

It was almost an hour before Ralph called back.

"Lisa," he said. "Please don't tell me you want the painting back. I love it. And I gave you a good price."

"No no," said Lisa. "There's no problem about the painting. You will think this is very strange, but I am looking for Gerry Wallace."

"Gerry Wallace? Why? I don't understand."

"It's a long story and it's hard to explain.," said Lisa.

"Can we meet for lunch? You can tell me all about it," answered Ralph.

"OK," said Lisa. "Where? When?"

"There's a nice café next door to the gallery. I could meet you there at twelve. Would that work for you?"

"Sure," said Lisa. "See you there."

Lisa felt excited. She sent a text to Gabby.

--- *I'm meeting Ralph, the guy from the art gallery for lunch. He knows something about Gerry Wallace. Tell you about it when I get back.* ---

Gabby answered immediately. --- *A date! Good for you!* ---

Oh Gabby, thought Lisa. *It's not a date. I'm just doing some detective work.*

Even though it wasn't a date, Lisa searched through her bathroom

The Box

cabinet and found some old mascara and a lipstick. She made up her face as best she could. She changed the pink T-shirt she was wearing for a blue one so she could wear the new silk scarf. She transferred everything from her old brown handbag to the white and gold one Yvonne had given her. She put the photograph and newspaper story from the box into an envelope, and put the envelope inside her new bag as well. She was ready to go.

Ralph was waiting at a table inside the café. He smiled as Lisa joined him. He handed her a menu. "I like the food here," he said. "Have you eaten here before?"

Lisa didn't want to tell him that she had only started going to cafes since her marriage broke up. And then it had only been twice, both times with Gabby.

She looked at the menu. "No, I haven't been here before. The food looks interesting."

"What will you have?" asked Ralph.

"Mmm. I'm going to have the corn fritters."

Ralph stood up. "I think I'll have the same. Tea or coffee?"

"Coffee, a latte."

Ralph went to the counter to order and pay.

Lisa was embarrassed. When he came back she said, "I didn't realise you had to order and pay at the same time. She opened her bag and took out her wallet. Please let me pay for my meal and yours too. You are here to help me!"

Ralph put his hand on Lisa's. "No. I invited you. I want to have lunch with you."

"But...."

"Forget it," laughed Ralph. "Now tell me the story."

Lisa explained about her mother's death and the box.

"I'm sure she wanted to tell me something, or show me something. But it was too late. She was dying and she couldn't speak. She just said one word – 'sorry'."

"So what did you find in the box?" asked Ralph.

"My aunt showed me how to open the secret drawer. There was a photograph and a newspaper story in it."

Lisa opened the envelope and put the items in front of Ralph.

"I searched for Gerry Wallace on the Internet. There was a photograph of him in a group. You were in the group too. So that's why I called you."

Ralph didn't say anything for a while. Then he said, "And you want to find Gerry Wallace because….?"

"I don't know. Because my mother wanted me to? Maybe she didn't. Maybe I am wrong. But it seems like it's the right thing to do."

Ralph took Lisa's hands across the table. "Sometimes when we search into the past, we find out things we would rather not know. It might make you unhappy. And I wouldn't like that."

Lisa was shocked. She stared at Ralph. His eyes were very sad. "Do you know something bad about this Gerry Wallace?"

"No. I don't. I'm sorry. I was thinking about my own experience. I'll tell you sometime."

Their meals arrived, and Ralph handed the photograph and newspaper article back to Lisa.

While they ate, Ralph talked about Lisa's picture. "I've hung it in my living room. It looks great. You must come and see it sometime. My friends will all be jealous. Where did you buy it?"

"Oh. It was many years ago. The artist had a caravan down by the beach at Waikanae. He was selling his paintings from the caravan. I saw it. I liked it. So I bought it."

"You were interested in art?"

"Yes I was. I was a student, so I had very little money. But I bought a few pictures. The others are hanging in my apartment. There was no room for the one you bought."

"I'd love to come and see what else you have," smiled Ralph.

Is he interested in me? Lisa felt strange. *He is being so friendly and kind. He said I should see the painting in his house. No. No. He's an art dealer. I guess he is wondering if I have any other paintings that are good.*

15. AN APOLOGY

When they finished eating, the waiter took their plates away and brought their coffees.

"I saw the group photograph on Elizabeth Benson's Facebook page. I was surprised it was open to the public. Don't most people have a 'friends only' block?" Lisa wanted to find out what Ralph knew about Gerry Wallace.

Ralph laughed. "I have known Elizabeth for many years. She's an amazing person. She would say, 'I have no secrets'. Of course that isn't true. I am sure she has many secrets, but I'm not surprised her Facebook page is public. Tell me about the photograph you saw."

"Sorry. I should have printed a copy, but I don't have a printer. There was a group of people. It looked like a BBQ party. The description said 'Reunion party, Summer 2017'. You were one of the people in the picture."

"Yes, I remember. But Lisa, I'm sorry. I was at the party. I was in the photograph, but I wasn't part of the reunion. I was having a hard time. I went to visit Elizabeth, but she was having a party. I wanted to leave, but Elizabeth made me stay. It wasn't my reunion and I didn't know any of the other people."

"Oh, no!" Lisa was disappointed. "So you don't know anything about Gerry Wallace!"

"I remember a little. He was a very quiet guy. Very nice person. The other people there talked a lot. He didn't say much.

"They had all worked together a long time before. And Elizabeth wanted to have a reunion. Where's that newspaper story?"

Lisa handed it to Ralph. "Maybe this was the project they all worked on. I don't know. Elizabeth has always done social work of one kind or another," he said.

He smiled at Lisa. "Why don't I take you to visit her? We could have lunch somewhere, and then call in on Elizabeth. Tomorrow?"

Lisa panicked. *This is all going too fast for me. I don't know this man. I'm not sure I want to find out about Gerry Wallace.*

She picked up her bag and put the newspaper story back in it.

"Thank you. But I don't think so. I need to think about it. Let me pay you for my lunch." She gave Ralph $20 and stood up. "Thank you for meeting me."

She walked out of the café. She stood outside. Her face was red. She felt shaky.

"Lisa! What's wrong?" Ralph had followed her out of the café.

"I'm sorry," said Lisa. "Things have been difficult lately. I don't want to talk about it." She walked past Ralph and hurried to her car.

Lisa sat in her car with her hands over her face.

You are such an idiot, she said to herself. *He was only being nice. And you were so rude!*

She heard someone tapping on the car window. *Oh, no! It's him. He followed me!*

She took her hands off her face. It was Aunt Yvonne.

Yvonne opened the passenger door and got into the car.

"I was coming back from the bank, when I saw you running down the street. What is the matter?"

Lisa sighed. She didn't want to talk about it. But she knew her aunt very well. Yvonne wouldn't give up until she had the whole story.

Lisa told Yvonne everything. "I don't know why I panicked," she said finally. "I am such a fool."

Yvonne sighed. "I don't know Ralph Watt, but I know his parents. I have seen him a few times when I've been to his gallery. He is a very attractive man, and he seems very nice. So what's the problem? I wonder if you really don't want to find out about Gerry Wallace? Or is it that you think Ralph is interested in you, and you're not interested in him?"

Lisa bit her lip. "I like him very much. He seems very kind and nice. But I don't know anything about men. Think about Darryl. He was having an affair for months and I had no idea. I was thinking he was the perfect husband. I don't want to get hurt again. And I am not sure I will be happy if I find Gerry Wallace. I'm scared."

Yvonne laughed. "Of course you're scared. But that's why you should accept Ralph's invitation and find Gerry Wallace. All the years you lived with Darryl, he decided everything. It's time for you to act like an adult. It's time for you to take risks."

"How?" Lisa thought Yvonne made everything sound very easy. But it wasn't.

"Well first, you are going to see Ralph and apologise."

"No!"

"Yes!" said Yvonne. "You asked him for help. He was trying to help you and you walked out of the restaurant. I think you should accept his offer to take you to meet Elizabeth. But even if you don't want to do that, you will have to say sorry. Grow up, Lisa! Darryl might have hurt you. But you have to move on. Don't let Darryl affect your life. Call him now."

"Uh. I'll do it later," said Lisa.

"No, Lisa. Now. I'm not getting out of this car until you make the call."

Lisa sighed. She found the art gallery number on her phone and called.

Ralph answered the phone.

"This is Lisa. I'm sorry I was so rude. I behaved very badly."

"I think you have some problems to sort out," answered Ralph. His voice sounded cold.

"Yes. I do. But my problems are no reason to be rude. Is the invitation to visit Elizabeth still open? It was very kind of you to offer to take me."

"I guess so." Ralph didn't sound very friendly. "Meet me at the gallery at ten thirty tomorrow morning."

"Thank you. I'll be there. And Ralph, I am very sorry."

"It's OK. See you tomorrow." Ralph hung up.

"Well done!" said Yvonne. "You did it."

Lisa stared at her aunt. "Yes. But he didn't sound very friendly."

"Of course not. Why should he? Tomorrow is another day. Wear something pretty and be nice to him." Yvonne got out of the car.

As she closed the door she said, "And don't even think about not going!"

16. AN UNEXPECTED PRESENT

Lisa went home. She felt very strange.

I don't know what is happening with my life. Maybe I have to find out about Gerry Wallace before I can organise my life. Is there a mystery? My family was so normal. It wasn't a family with secrets.

Lisa thought about her father. He had died in a car accident when she was 20.

That was while I was still at university, and not long before I met Darryl, and got married. I wonder if my life would be different if he hadn't got killed. He was such a quiet man. He never said anything much, but he was a very good and kind father. I wonder what he would have said about Darryl. Would he have liked him?

Her phone beeped. It was a text from Gabby.

--- *How was your lunch date? Shall I come down for a coffee?* ---

--- *It wasn't a date. But yes. Come! I have a lot to tell you.* ---

Gabby came into the apartment about ten minutes later. She was carrying a paper bag.

"Three cheese muffins. I was working hard, and I didn't eat lunch. You can have one and I'll have two. Now tell me everything!"

They drank coffee and ate the muffins while Lisa told Gabby about the lunch, the invitation, and how she had run out of the café.

Gabby watched Lisa carefully when she talked about panicking and running away. "Why did you do that?"

"I don't know. It's not long since my husband walked out on me. And I had no idea he had another woman in his life. Maybe I'm scared."

The Box

"Yes. You think Ralph is interested in you, but maybe it is the other way around. Maybe you are interested in him, and he is just being kind and friendly. You don't know. You are thinking too much. Just relax and see what happens." Gabby stood up. "I have to go. I have so much work to do. But before I go, please show me what you are going to wear tomorrow."

"It doesn't matter. All my new clothes are great."

"Ah, yes, they are. But you want something special for tomorrow. It will give you confidence."

Lisa showed Gabby the bag and scarf that Yvonne had given her.

"Lucky you!" smiled Gabby. "Let's find an outfit to go with the bag."

After Gabby left, Lisa poured herself a glass of wine and read a magazine.

Late in the afternoon the doorbell rang. She opened the door. A bicycle courier was standing outside holding a box. "This is for you," he said. "Please sign here."

"Thank you," she said. "But I wasn't expecting a delivery. Who is it from?"

"I picked it up from Yvonne's. The dress shop. My girlfriend would love to shop there. But it's too expensive."

"Too expensive for me too," smiled Lisa.

"Well, maybe someone's giving you a present."

Lisa signed for the delivery, and the bicycle courier ran down the stairs.

Lisa put the box on the table and went to the kitchen to find scissors to open it.

It's from Aunt Yvonne. I wonder what it is?

She opened the box. Oh, Aunt Yvonne! You are amazing!

The box was filled with cosmetics.

Lisa picked up her phone and sent a text to Yvonne.

--- *Thank you for the amazing present!* ---

An answer came back very quickly.

--- *Make sure you use them tomorrow. Good luck.* ---

17. ELIZABETH

The next morning, Lisa dressed and spent almost 40 minutes putting on her new makeup. It took her a long time because she had not used much makeup for a long time.

Finally, she was happy. *I think I look OK. My clothes are nice, my hair looks good and the makeup helps too. I feel more confident.*

As she was leaving the apartment, she looked at the box. She opened the secret drawer and took out the little brass ring. She put it on her finger, picked up her bag and hurried out of the house.

Ralph was waiting outside the gallery. He smiled at Lisa.

"My car is over there," he said pointing to a very new-looking BMW. "Shall we go?"

He held the door open for Lisa and she got in the car.

They didn't talk at all for a few minutes as Ralph drove through the traffic and out onto the motorway.

Then Ralph said. "Did I upset you yesterday, when I said you might find out things about your past that would upset you?"

"Maybe a little," said Lisa. "But I still want to know. I was rude yesterday. So I have to explain something about myself." She told Ralph about Darryl leaving her just after her mother died. She told him about Kathy, the secret girlfriend, and the baby that Kathy and Darryl were expecting.

"So I'm feeling very strange at the moment. I have to make a new life for myself. Sometimes it seems too much, and I get scared."

"That's not surprising," said Ralph. "You have had a very hard time. And then, there is this mystery about Gerry Wallace. I hope you can get some answers. But, I also hope you won't find out anything that would make you unhappy."

Lisa thought Ralph might explain about his own bad experience, but he didn't.

It's none of my business, she thought. *If he wanted to tell me, he would say something.*

Lisa enjoyed the drive to Raumati. They arrived at Elizabeth's house just after 11:00. It was an old cottage with a beautiful garden. A woman wearing a big sunhat and gardening gloves, was standing by the gate when Ralph stopped the car.

He got out of the car and walked towards her. They hugged and then Ralph turned back to Lisa.

"Elizabeth. This is Lisa. She wants to know about Gerry Wallace."

"Yes," said Elizabeth. "You told me on the phone. Welcome, my dear. I will do what I can to help you. Come into the house."

Elizabeth took them into the house. "Come into the kitchen," she said. "I'll make some tea."

Ralph and Lisa sat at the kitchen table. Lisa watched Elizabeth as she made tea. She was quite old, and very fat. Her long white hair was tied up in a knot on top of her head, and she was wearing a long purple and yellow dress.

Elizabeth brought teacups and a plate of shortbread to the table. She sat down opposite Lisa and said, "Now, tell me the story."

Lisa explained about her mother, the box, the newspaper story, and the photograph. She told Elizabeth about the Internet search and the photograph on Elizabeth's Facebook page.

Then she said, "Of course there might be no connection at all. The Gerry Wallace you know might not be the same person. Would you look at the photograph please?"

She took the photograph out of her bag, and handed it to Elizabeth. The elderly woman took the photograph, but she didn't look at it. She stared at Lisa's hand.

"I don't need to look at the photograph," she said. "That ring you are wearing. Was it with the photograph?"

"Yes," said Lisa. "It was in the box."

"Gerry has a ring exactly the same," said Elizabeth slowly. "He always wears it. So I am sure he is the person you are looking for."

She reached across the table and took Lisa's hands. Lisa stared at her. Elizabeth had very beautiful, dark brown eyes. Her eyes were very kind.

"Are you sure you want to meet him?" she asked.

"I'm not sure. But I think so. My mother was trying to tell me something. I think I have to do this for her."

Elizabeth let go of Lisa's hands and sat back in her chair.

"He has always been a very sad man. I think there is something in his past that makes him unhappy. Maybe it will make you unhappy too."

"I understand," said Lisa. "But I want to see him. Do you think he will agree to meet me?"

"I don't know," answered Elizabeth. "What can you tell me about Gerry and your mother?"

"Not very much. They dated at university. They dropped out of university and went to India. Then my mother came back to New Zealand with my father. She was pregnant. They got married, and I was born. I only know this because my aunt told me. She didn't know anything else. She wasn't living in this area then. And neither my mother, nor my father, ever told me anything about going to India. Maybe my parents met in some other place."

"Mmmm," Elizabeth looked thoughtful. "I don't want to upset Gerry. He is a very old friend, and a good man. I want to talk to him first. I will ask him if he wants to meet you. It might be a few days. Sometimes he is hard to find. Do you mind waiting?"

"No," said Lisa. "It is very kind of you to help me. If he says 'no', it will be OK. I will have tried my best for my mother."

Elizabeth stood up. "I have to go to meet my husband. He is working at the youth centre today. I must go to help cook lunch for the young people. Give me your phone number. I'll call you when I have some news."

Lisa gave Elizabeth the number.

"Thank you for seeing me," she said.

Lisa and Ralph stood up, and they walked with Elizabeth to the door.

Elizabeth stopped and took Ralph's hands. She looked up at him and said. "Ralph, are you doing OK?"

"Yes. I'm much better now, Elizabeth. Some days I feel bad, but I'm learning to live with it."

"Good," said Elizabeth. "You know that nothing that happened was your fault. You must keep telling yourself that."

"I will."
Elizabeth stood and waved as Ralph and Lisa drove away.

18. RALPH'S STORY

"I thought we could go to a café down by the beach," said Ralph. "Would that be OK? Or would you rather go straight back?"

"No. I'd love to have lunch. And I promise you I won't run away this time!" answered Lisa. "I'm worried though. You are taking a lot of time from your work for me."

Ralph laughed. "I am the owner! I can do what I like. And I want to do this."

The café Ralph chose was almost on the beach. They sat outside and looked at the sea. They ordered fish and chips. It was a weekday, so there were only local people in the street.

They talked about art and music. Lisa told Ralph about her Aunt Yvonne, and how bossy she was. "But she was very kind to me after my mother died," said Lisa. "I don't know what I would have done without her."

"I know who she is," said Ralph. "She is a very clever businesswoman. My parents know her."

Suddenly, Ralph's mood seemed to change.

"I'll go and pay the bill," he said. He stood up and walked back into the café.

He seems very angry, thought Lisa. *What did I do wrong? What did I say?*

Ralph came back. "Shall we go for a walk?"

"OK." Lisa felt nervous.

They left the restaurant and walked across the road and onto the beach. Ralph walked very fast, and Lisa found it hard to walk at the same pace.

The Box

"Ralph," she said. "Did I do something wrong? You seem very angry."

Ralph stopped walking. He looked at Lisa.

"No. You didn't do anything wrong. It's me. Sometimes, I am not a good person to be with."

Lisa thought about what Elizabeth had said when they were leaving her house. *You know that nothing that happened was your fault. You must keep telling yourself that.*

"Did you have some bad experience in your past?" she asked.

Ralph took Lisa's hand. "I have only talked to my parents and Elizabeth about this. No one else knows. But I want to tell you. Let's sit down. He pulled Lisa over to a piece of wood. They sat down, and Ralph let go of Lisa's hand. He stared at the sea and started talking.

"I have wonderful parents. I had a wonderful childhood. When I wanted to start a business, my parents gave me the money. I have had a very lucky life.

"I was adopted. I always knew that. But it was OK. I knew my adoptive parents loved me, and I love them. Then, one night last year, I was visiting them. We had dinner and were watching the news on TV. There was a news item about a drug war. A man had been shot in the street. They showed his picture on the TV, and it was me!"

"What?" Lisa was shocked.

"Well, no. It wasn't me. The hair was different. The clothes were different. He looked ill. He looked older than me. But he looked so much like me!

"My parents and I were amazed. We talked about it. My father said 'They told us your mother was a drug addict. They told us she could not look after you.'

"My mother cried. 'We wanted you so much. If you had had a brother we would have adopted him too.'

"Then my father said. 'You must find out. You will never be happy until you know if the man who was killed, was your brother. Ask Elizabeth to help you. She knows a lot about these things. And we will help you as much as we can'."

Lisa took Ralph's hand and held it tightly. "Your parents are amazing people. What happened?" she asked.

"Elizabeth helped me. It took a long time. But finally, we learned everything. The story about my mother was very bad. She was a drug addict. She had two children. My brother, and me. But Lisa! We were twins! The man who was killed was my twin brother! The social workers tried to take both of us from her. But she said, 'I want one child'. So the social workers chose me.

"My twin brother had a terrible life. There was no money. My mother died. He lived on the streets. He was always in trouble with the police. He had nothing, and I had everything.

"My parents are rich. I went to the best schools. I went on vacation to amazing places. My parents bought me a car when I graduated from high school. And all the time I was having this amazing life, my brother was poor and hungry!"

Lisa felt very sad. *I think my life is bad. My husband left me. He will have a child with another woman. But that is nothing. I understand how Ralph must feel. I don't know what to say.*

Then she said. "What was his name? What was your brother's name?"

Ralph sighed. "Oh, Lisa. Thank you for asking. Even if he had a sad life, he was a real person. His name was Leon."

Ralph stood up. "I'm sorry. I want to leave now."

"Yes, of course."

They walked back to the car without speaking.

Ralph drove back to the city. He didn't say anything.

Ralph didn't speak until they were in the city. "Where do you live?' he asked.

Lisa gave him the address, and Ralph drove to her apartment block.

When Ralph stopped the car, Lisa said, "Thank you for today. I understand now, why you said that when we search into the past, we might discover things we would rather not know. But I heard what Elizabeth said. I think she is a very wise woman. You did not make these things happen. It was not your fault."

Ralph reached across and hugged Lisa. "I think that I was very lucky to meet you."

19. WAITING

Lisa went up to her apartment. It was only 4:30pm, but she was very tired. She lay down on her small sofa. She looked at her smartphone. *Gabby and Aunt Yvonne have sent messages. But I don't want to answer them right now,* she thought. *They are very energetic, successful women. I need some rest. It is all too much for me.*

Lisa found the next two days difficult. She stayed in her apartment. Aunt Yvonne sent text messages. Lisa answered them --- *I'm fine. Everything is good.* ---

It was a busy time of year for Yvonne, so she thought, *Lisa is OK. I don't need to worry.*

Gabby was also very busy, but she came down for coffee. Lisa was pleased to see her, but she didn't talk very much. Gabby was worried. Lisa seemed tired. She wasn't interested in anything.

On the third day, Gabby left Lisa's apartment and went downtown. She went to Yvonne's boutique. She asked to speak to Yvonne.

Yvonne came out from the back of the store. "Can I help you?" she asked.

"Oh, you don't know me. I'm Gabby. I live upstairs from your niece, Lisa. "

Yvonne smiled. "Gabby! So nice to meet you! You have been so kind to Lisa. But why are you here?"

"I am worried about Lisa," said Gabby.

"Give me five minutes!" said Yvonne. "Look around the shop. We will go out for coffee."

Gabby looked at the clothes in Yvonne's boutique. *Wow!* she thought. *These clothes are amazing. I love them. But one outfit would cost more than I spend on clothes in a year!*

Yvonne came back, and she walked with Gabby to a nearby café.

They sat down and ordered coffees. Yvonne said, "Put them on my account."

"You have been a very good friend to Lisa," said Yvonne while they waited for their coffees. "Tell me why you are worried."

Gabby shrugged. "I don't know. Lisa went for lunch with Ralph, the guy from the art gallery. I think maybe it did not go well. The next day she went with him, to see a woman who might know something about the mystery man – Gerry Wallace. Since then, she has been very stressed. Lisa has had such a hard time. She won't talk about what happened. I don't know if she heard something bad about Gerry Wallace, or if she is having problems with Ralph. I think he likes her very much."

Their coffees arrived and Yvonne drank a little before she answered Gabby. "Have you met Ralph?"

"No," said Gabby. "I know about his art gallery. It is very successful."

"Of course you never met Darryl, Lisa's husband."

"No. And I don't want to. I think he is a selfish rat!" said Gabby.

Yvonne laughed. "He is not a very nice man. Very boring. And yes, I agree. He is very selfish. I don't know why Lisa married him. He took everything from her. She had no life, no fun. Now, Ralph. I have often seen him. I know his parents. They have a lot of money. He is a very attractive man. And I think he is interested in Lisa."

"So what is the problem?" asked Gabby. "Attractive, rich guy. Why is Lisa so worried?"

"I think there are two problems. Lisa doesn't know how to react to a man being interested in her. She likes him, but she can't believe he likes her. Darryl always told her she was not attractive, she was not clever. She believed him."

"Then the other problem is her mother and the mystery man – Gerry Wallace."

Gabby and Yvonne drank their coffees in silence. Then Yvonne said, "This is difficult. Lisa asked me about Alice, her mother, and Gerry Wallace. I didn't tell Lisa very much. But I remember they were very much in love. When Alice came back from India with Alan, I was very surprised. She was pregnant with Lisa. Then, Alice and Alan got married. Later, Lisa was born. I liked Alan very much. He was a very nice man. A good husband and a good father, but I always thought there was something wrong."

Gabby looked at her phone. "I have to go. I have deadlines. Lisa seems to be waiting for something. What can I do to help her?"

"I don't know," Yvonne looked tired and old. "I loved my sister, Alice. I promised her I would look after her daughter. But, I am better at business than looking after people."

Gabby laughed. "You are very good at business, but I think you have also done a lot for Lisa."

"I like your style," said Yvonne. "I am thinking about online sales for my company. Lisa says you are a website designer. We should talk."

"Another day," said Gabby. "I am always looking for new clients. But today I have to look after the clients I already have. See you later!"

20. A PLAN FOR THE MEETING

While Gabby and Yvonne were drinking coffee, Elizabeth called Lisa.

"Lisa," she said. "I talked to Gerry. I called him the same day you came to see me. He said he didn't know if he wanted to meet you. He said he wanted to think about it. Today he called me back."

"What did he say?" asked Lisa.

"He said he will meet you. He said he wants to tell you a story. I said you could meet at my house. But he said 'no'. I don't know why, but he wants to meet you some other place. He does not want me to be there."

"Why?" Lisa felt nervous. Elizabeth was Gerry Wallace's friend. Lisa did not understand.

"Lisa, I don't know. But I have arranged a meeting. Gerry Wallace will meet you in Ralph's apartment. I think this is good. I don't know what Gerry will tell you, but, if Ralph is there, you will have support."

"No!" said Lisa. "Ralph had a bad time! I don't want him to have more stress!"

Elizabeth didn't say anything for a short time. Then she said, "Ralph told you about his brother?"

"Yes he did. It was so hard for him. I think it is still hard for him." Lisa was upset.

"Listen to me, Lisa," said Elizabeth. "Ralph told you about his brother. He trusts you. So please trust him. It is very important. Tomorrow at eleven am, Ralph will meet Gerry at the railway station. He will take him to his apartment. You will be there. You will listen to Gerry's story."

"But, but ….." It was no good. Elizabeth had hung up.

Lisa decided she would not tell Gabby or Aunt Yvonne about the meeting.

They will have a lot of advice for me, she thought. *They will be too interested in what I am going to wear. They will be surprised that I am going to Ralph's apartment. I will tell them after it is all over.*

A little later, the phone rang again. It was Ralph. "Did Elizabeth call you?" he asked.

"Yes she did," answered Lisa. "She told me the plan. But I don't like it. It seems strange."

"I think so too," said Ralph. "But Elizabeth asked me to invite you and Gerry Wallace to my apartment. She said she couldn't think of another plan."

"But why not a café? It seems strange."

"I said the same thing to Elizabeth. She said Gerry wouldn't meet you in a public place. She was worried. That's why she asked me. I always help Elizabeth when I can. She has been very kind to me."

Lisa sighed. "OK. But I was nervous before. Now I feel a little scared."

"Don't worry. I will be there. I will come to your apartment building at ten fifteen. We will go to my apartment. And anyway, there is a bonus!"

"A bonus?"

"You will see how great your picture looks on my wall! I have to go. So tomorrow, at ten fifteen?"

"OK, and thank you."

Lisa couldn't sleep that night. She felt restless and uncertain.

What have I done? she asked herself. *I started this search and now I think it was a bad idea. I wish I could stop, but it's too late now.*

Finally, she fell asleep. When she woke up, it was 9:00am. She felt stronger and more confident.

I will find out today what the mystery is, and then it will all be over. I can start living my new life.

At 10:15am, Lisa was waiting outside her apartment building. She had the newspaper article and photograph in her bag, and she was wearing the ring from the box. She didn't know if it was a good idea to wear it, but she wanted to know about it.

Ralph arrived on time. "Good morning! How are you feeling?" he asked, as Lisa got in the car.

"Better today," she smiled. "I panicked yesterday but then, this morning, I thought I will have the answer to the mystery very soon. That will be a good thing."

They drove to Ralph's apartment. It was in a block of luxury apartments.

They took the elevator to the top floor. Ralph unlocked the door and Lisa walked in. "Oh!" she said. The apartment was very modern and very beautiful. It was open plan. The kitchen, dining area and living area were all in one huge room. One wall was all glass. There were wonderful views out over the harbour. "It's amazing!"

Ralph gently turned Lisa away from the view, and pointed to the wall above the dining table. "Your picture," he said. "It looks good, doesn't it?"

Lisa stared at the picture. "I understand why you wanted it," she said softly. "It belongs here."

"I have to go to the railway station now," said Ralph. "Maybe you could make some coffee? You'll find everything in the kitchen. See you soon."

Lisa went to the kitchen and found Ralph's coffeemaker. She found coffee, sugar, cream and cups. She switched the coffeemaker on and walked back over to the windows. Outside, was a balcony with a table and chairs.

Maybe we can sit out there, she thought.

She heard the door to the apartment open, and turned around. Her heart was beating quickly.

She heard Ralph saying, "Well here we are, Gerry. And here is Lisa."

21. GERRY'S STORY

The man who walked into the apartment with Ralph looked nervous. Ralph was smiling, but Gerry looked as scared as Lisa felt.

"Why don't you sit out on the balcony?" said Ralph. "I see Lisa has made coffee. I'll bring it out to you."

Lisa and Gerry sat on the balcony in silence. Ralph bought out a tray of coffee. He bent down and kissed Lisa's cheek. "I'll be inside if you need me."

Lisa poured coffee and passed a cup to Gerry. He cleared his throat. "Thank you," he said. "Ralph seems like a nice guy."

"Yes, he is," said Lisa. "He is a very nice man."

"And you met Elizabeth?"

"Yes. Ralph took me to visit her."

"And Alice's husband, Alan. Was he a nice man? Did you have a good childhood?"

"Yes. I did. My father was a very quiet man. He was always kind to me."

Lisa was wondering what these questions were about.

"Good. Good. And he died?"

"Yes. A long time ago."

"And Alice. Your mother. Elizabeth told me she died only a few months ago."

"Yes," said Lisa. "It was a very difficult time for me."

Gerry stared out at the ocean. "You are wearing Alice's ring. I gave that to her. I gave it to her on the day we got married."

"Married! You were married to my mother?"

"I don't think it was a real marriage. I mean, I don't think it was legal. We were young, and in love. We didn't sign any papers, but we said it was a wedding. We were in Goa. It was on the beach. We had friends and flowers and a party. Some old guy who lived on the beach said he could do a ceremony. I still wear the ring she gave me that day. But then…."

"What do you mean? But then…"

Gerry turned and looked at Lisa. He looked very old and sad. "I don't want to tell you this part of the story, but I must. Very soon after the wedding, Alice found out that she was pregnant. I loved the lifestyle we had. I didn't want it to change. But Alice changed. She wanted to have the baby. I didn't. I was very young and selfish. And I had no money, and no way of caring for a wife and a baby. I loved Alice, but there was no room in my life for a baby. I wanted someone who would party, and travel, and do crazy things. Alice said there was no way she would do that with a young child. We talked about it. Alice would not give up the baby. I didn't want a baby.

"We made a plan. There was a guy we knew. His name was Alan. He was a very nice, quiet guy. We thought he liked Alice very much. Alice went to him. She said that we had broken up. Alan was pleased, I think. Alice told him she wanted to be with him. I went away to Nepal, and Alice stayed with Alan."

"I was that baby!"

"Yes. You were that baby. And I am so sorry! I went to Nepal, but as soon as I got there, I realised I had made a terrible mistake. But it was too late. I had persuaded Alice to go to another man with my child. I could not go back."

Lisa was finding it difficult to breathe. "Did Alan know I was not his child?"

"I don't know," said Gerry. "I never saw or spoke to Alice again. But Alan was a very nice man. Maybe he knew you were not his child, but he loved Alice. So maybe it was OK. But you must believe me. I have thought about my child and the mistakes I made, every day for forty years. I am so ashamed."

Lisa felt sick to her stomach. Her head hurt. She tried hard to get some control. She looked at Gerry. He looked sick and tired. His face was grey, and his hands were shaking.

It is a terrible story, she thought. *Did this man and my mother trick Alan? Did Alan think I was his child? It was so unkind. I must show respect to*

Alan.

"I don't know if Alan knew I was not his daughter," she said softly and slowly. "But I do know that he was proud of me. He loved me. I was his daughter – in a real way - because he was there for me every day of our family life. Alan and Alice and me – we were a family. He was my father. Not you. You walked away from me. You cannot say I am your daughter. You are nothing to me, and I want nothing to do with you."

22. SHOCKED

Lisa walked back into the apartment, then she lost control. She ran to the door. Her only thought was to escape. She wanted to be as far away from this man, who called himself her father, as she could. But Ralph was too quick for her.

He stood in front of the door. "No, Lisa," he said. "You can't do this."

Lisa was very angry. She punched Ralph again and again with her fists. "Get out of my way!"

Ralph grabbed Lisa's wrists and held them. "No Lisa," he said again. "This is not the way."

Lisa fell against Ralph's chest. He put his arms around her. She cried and cried. After a short time, she calmed down. Ralph led her to the sofa.

"Sit down," he said. He handed her a box of tissues and left the room. When he came back, he was carrying a wet facecloth. He wiped her face. He took the facecloth away and returned to sit next to her.

"Where's Gerry?" asked Lisa.

"He's still sitting on the balcony," answered Ralph.

"I feel terrible," said Lisa. "I am an adult woman, but I behaved like a child. It was such a shock."

"It's OK," said Ralph. "It was a shock for you. I am sure Gerry will understand."

"Do I have to talk to him?" Lisa asked childishly.

"Yes. Of course you do," said Ralph. "You went looking for him.

The Box

You wanted to know the story. He didn't want to tell you, but he did. He told you because you wanted to know. It was painful for you, but think. It must have been very difficult for him. I'm going to ask him to come in."

Ralph went onto the balcony and spoke to Gerry for a few minutes. Then the two men came into the apartment.

Ralph went into the kitchen and Gerry sat down in an armchair facing Lisa.

"I'm sorry…" they both said together.

"I'm sorry," Lisa started again. "I got a shock, and I was very rude. I understand it was very difficult for you to come here today."

"Yes, it was," said Gerry. "You are my daughter and I want you to think well of me. But how can you? I did a terrible thing."

Lisa didn't speak for a while, but then she said, "I am trying to understand. You were very young."

"Yes. I was young, and I was selfish. I didn't want to change my lifestyle. But I was frightened too. I could hardly look after myself. I didn't believe I could look after Alice and a child. So I ran away. Only a few days later, I realised I had made a terrible mistake. But by then it was too late. I did a terrible thing to Alan too."

"No," said Lisa quietly. Then she said in a stronger voice, "Alice, my mother, was also part of what happened. She agreed to go to Alan. To tell Alan that you had broken up. But perhaps it was not so bad. I think Alice and Alan were happy together. I had a very good childhood. Alan was a good father. It was only after Alan died, that things went bad for me."

"What happened?" asked Gerry.

Lisa told Gerry about Darryl. "After my mother died, and he left me, I thought my world had ended. But now, I know it was the best thing that could have happened. I had no life when I lived with Darryl. He controlled everything I did, and he took away all my self-confidence. He never allowed me to have friends, or to go to work, or to have money of my own. Now I have new friends. Thanks to Ralph, I have some money. I can plan my future. It is good."

Ralph came back with a bottle of wine and glasses.

"I think we all need this," he said smiling.

Ralph sat down next to Lisa and served the wine.

Gerry drank some wine and then said, "I would like to be part of your new life, Lisa. But I guess that is impossible. Alice made a new life with Alan, and she forgot about me. I think it is best if you forget about me too."

"But no!" said Lisa. "She wanted me to know about you. She never forgot you! When she was dying, she wanted to tell me, but it was too late. But she wanted me to have the box. She had kept the ring and the photograph. She cut the article about you out of the newspaper. She wanted me to meet you!"

Gerry's eyes filled with tears. "I don't deserve to be happy, but today I am."

23. FOUR MONTHS LATER

A group of people walked across the lawns of the city graveyard. It was a beautiful day. Lisa and Ralph were holding hands. Gerry, Yvonne, Elizabeth and her husband, were with them. Everyone was carrying flowers.

They went first to Leon's grave.

"Who was he?" asked Gerry. "Tell me about him."

"He was my twin brother," said Ralph. "He had a sad life. I didn't know anything about him until after he died. He was buried in Auckland. But I was able to have his ashes moved here, so I could visit him sometimes."

Ralph and Lisa put flowers on Leon's grave. Then they all walked to where Alan and Alice were buried together.

Yvonne and Lisa put flowers for Alan and Alice, and then it was Gerry's turn.

He put a single rose on the grave, and then he spoke. "I never thought this could happen, Alice. We could never be together in life, but I can visit your grave with our daughter. It should be sad. But somehow it is happy. Thank you, Alan, for caring for Lisa. Thank you Alice, for making it possible for Lisa to discover our secret. Lisa is living with Ralph now. She has a talent for discovering art, so she is working with him in his gallery. I see her often. The future looks good."

I Talk You Talk Press

THANK YOU

Thank you for reading The Box. (Word count: 16,728) We hope you enjoyed Lisa's story.

If you would like to read more graded readers, please visit our website http://www.italkyoutalk.com

Other Level 4 graded readers include
Chi-obaa and Friends
Chi-obaa and Her Town
End House (Old Secrets – Modern Mysteries Book 2)
On the Run (Old Secrets – Modern Mysteries Book 3)
The Blue Lace Curtain (Old Secrets – Modern Mysteries Book 1)
The Legacy
The Witches of Nakashige
Vanished Away

ABOUT THE AUTHOR

I Talk You Talk Press is a Japan-based publisher of language textbooks, graded readers and language learning/teaching resources.

Our team is made up of highly experienced language teachers and translators, who have all studied at least one additional language to an advanced level.

This experience enables us to design our materials from the perspective of both the teacher and the learner. We consult with both teachers and language learners when designing our textbooks and graded readers, and test our materials extensively in the classroom before publication.

We are a fast-growing press, and currently publish graded readers for learners of English. We publish new graded readers monthly.

www.ingramcontent.com/pod-product-compliance
Lightning Source LLC
Chambersburg PA
CBHW032215040426
42449CB00005B/603